Life In Psalm

Live Where Faith and Your Story Intersect

Dearest A.J. Volunteer,
 May you experience blessing beyond expectation as you read this book.
  Psalm 28:7
   Andrea M Jerozal

ANDREA M JEROZAL

WESTBOW
PRESS®
A DIVISION OF THOMAS NELSON
& ZONDERVAN

Copyright © 2021 Andrea M Jerozal.

All rights reserved. No part of this book may be used or reproduced by any means, graphic, electronic, or mechanical, including photocopying, recording, taping or by any information storage retrieval system without the written permission of the author except in the case of brief quotations embodied in critical articles and reviews.

This book is a work of non-fiction. Unless otherwise noted, the author and the publisher make no explicit guarantees as to the accuracy of the information contained in this book and in some cases, names of people and places have been altered to protect their privacy.

WestBow Press books may be ordered through booksellers or by contacting:

WestBow Press
A Division of Thomas Nelson & Zondervan
1663 Liberty Drive
Bloomington, IN 47403
www.westbowpress.com
844-714-3454

Because of the dynamic nature of the Internet, any web addresses or links contained in this book may have changed since publication and may no longer be valid. The views expressed in this work are solely those of the author and do not necessarily reflect the views of the publisher, and the publisher hereby disclaims any responsibility for them.

Any people depicted in stock imagery provided by Getty Images are models, and such images are being used for illustrative purposes only. Certain stock imagery © Getty Images.

Interior Image Credit: Andrea Jerozal

Scripture quotations are from The ESV® Bible (The Holy Bible, English Standard Version®), copyright © 2001 by Crossway, a publishing ministry of Good News Publishers. Used by permission. All rights reserved.

ISBN: 978-1-6642-4202-9 (sc)
ISBN: 978-1-6642-4203-6 (hc)
ISBN: 978-1-6642-4201-2 (e)

Library of Congress Control Number: 2021915677

Print information available on the last page.

WestBow Press rev. date: 9/7/2021

Dedication

With Love from the depths of my heart to Jim, Jason & Angelyn -
> *You each inspire me and trigger my creativity. God is SO good to give me you.*

With Honor to John & Sandy Norris -
> *Parents bring life, love, coaching, prayers; all invaluable and treasured.*

With Gratitude to Jim and Elsie Jerozal -
> *Your support, love, prayer and welcome are irreplaceable.*

With Affection to my dear, precious friends -
> *Chloe, Kim A, Laurie, Kristi, Kim B, Amy A, Leslie O #1, Leslie O #2, Terran, Elizabeth & Amy S. You are the best – your love, prayers, heart-to-hearts, cheerleading, and celebrations!*

With Hope to all the unknown authors and poets out there -
> *God sees your every word and heart expression.*

Introduction

Dearest reader,

First, please know that in this book, freedom and grace are extended to you. You do not have to start at the beginning and read each page in sequence until the end, though you are free to! Reading through the table of contents, you will notice each modern psalm touches on a topic that may capture your attention based on what you are experiencing in life right now. Feel free to start there! Start at the last psalm and work your way backward if that suits your fancy. Enjoy!

*Second, I am not **ever** attempting to add to or replace Scripture. I use the word "psalm" to refer to poetry written from faith's life experience, perhaps with a hint of sing-song rhythm. David, the Biblical psalm writer, penned some of the most exquisite songs/poetry of all time and many of those words float around my brain daily and inspire me. Though I believe my words on the page to be Spirit-led and to not contradict God's Word, I am **not** a Bible writer. No-one past the writer of the book of Revelation is.*

*Third, piggybacking on the previous point, this book was written with an intention for each reader to engage in a new way with God's Word. The format is such that you can freshly discover how God addresses a wide variety of human emotion and experience. Read what **He** says and may He strengthen your faith and deepen intimacy with Him.*

Fourth, my kids have learned the value of "writing prompts" in school. Such a concept is probably familiar to most poets, songwriters and authors. This book may accompany your life for a time in your faith journey. It can serve as a series of writing prompts, releasing you to express your own thoughts and experiences in your unique way.

Fifth, if you are someone unconvinced about the reality and/or goodness of the God who calls Himself Yahweh, then perhaps this book may spark an appreciation for, or a hunger to better understand, the Biblical God many in this world follow.

Finally, thank you. Thank you for finding a few quiet moments in your life to sit down with these pages. Perhaps with a hot cup of coffee or chilly glass of iced tea, take a deep breath, and share some special time with God. I pray He ministers to your inner being.

Contents

1. Celebrate! 1
2. He Hears 5
3. Awe 8
4. Reverence 11
5. Beware Deception 14
6. Confession 18
7. Weariness 21
8. Divine Purpose 24
9. True Freedom 28
10. Warfare 31
11. Promises, promises 35
12. Unforeseen Storm 38
13. New Child Lullaby 43
14. Little Child Lullaby 46
15. Tween Lullaby 49
16. Orphan 54
17. Refugee 58
18. Find Me 63
19. Exposed 66
20. Surprising Joy 69
21. Grace 73
22. Trinity 76
23. The Great Rescue 79
24. Wrongly Accused 84
25. Where? 87
26. Best 90
27. Community 94
28. Dying Young 97
29. Unborn Life 101
30. Worship? 104
31. Child's Heart 107
32. In Progress 111

- **33.** So True 114
- **34.** Loss 117
- **35.** Overwhelmed 122
- **36.** Birthday Psalm 125
- **37.** Heaven's Not Here. 130
- **38.** Now 134
- **39.** Not Dead Yet 137
- **40.** Together 140
- **41.** Grief Delayed. 144
- **42.** Soul Talk 148
- **43.** Enemy Intention 152
- **44.** Modern Advent 155
- **45.** Ambush 158
- **46.** Restless. 161
- **47.** Identity. 164
- **48.** Friendship 167
- **49.** Kingdom Come 171
- **50.** Question Death 175
- **51.** Love Psalm. 181
- **52.** In the End. 186

Celebrate!

Let us celebrate our Lord God!
Let us fix our eyes with wonder
    upon our Lover who has no beginning or end.
Let us bow in His presence
    absorbing peace and relief for our hearts weary of sin.
Let us celebrate our Lord God!
Let us dance in the freedom
    He granted when he pardoned our souls.
Let us embrace and kiss one another
    to express gratitude for His great gifts.
Let us grasp each others hand and
    stand face to face gazing at His wonders.
Let us celebrate our Lord God!
Let us know laughter through tears
    of joy for His incomprehensible love.
Let us unify in partnership
    With all others who proclaim His truth.

"Celebrate" – original artwork by Andrea Jerozal
www.simplyhisstudiollc.com

Write out and then meditate on / contemplate:

Psalm 89:15,16; Psalm 106:1; Isaiah 63:7; Ephesians 5:18b-20

Journal Your Thoughts or Key Words/Phrases/Concepts:

*Write **your** psalm or prayer:*

He Hears

I praise You Lord because You heard my prayer.
When I was burdened by sadness
And what I could not understand
You answered my plea.

You have intervened, dear Lord, with Your truth.
At the level of my emotions
You lifted the heaviness of my heart
Troubled within me.

You acted with love according to my petition.
You bestowed to me a portion of grace
Generously measured from
Your immeasurable wealth.

You lightened my soul.
My fear, my sadness, my frustration
Replaced by Your peace, Your hope, Your patience for
You are their infinite source.

What other "god" accomplishes such things?
To transform a heart or renew a mind
With truth to refresh a worn-down soul.
Only **You**.
Only You.

Write out and then meditate on / contemplate:

Psalm 6:9; Psalm 66:16-20; I John 5:14

Journal Your Thoughts or Key Words/Phrases/Concepts:

*Write **your** psalm or prayer:*

Awe

The beauty of Your pure love is too wonderful for my mind and heart to absorb.
>My breath is taken from me.

The fire of Your holy, jealous love could consume us all and leave no trace.
>My soul trembles.

The depths of Your merciful love rescued me though snared in my own rebellion.
>My lips are silenced.

The demand of Your righteous love sacrificed Him who You loved first to pay for my evil.
>My knees buckle.

The endurance of Your strong love never weakens according to my deeds.
>My arms reach for You.

The hope of Your faithful love confidently awaits the day of Your perfection in me.
>My heart's strength is renewed.

You alone are truly God.
>There is no other that can compare to You.

Write out and then meditate on / contemplate:

Psalm 86:15-17; Psalm 106:1; Exodus 34:14

Journal Your Thoughts or Key Words/Phrases/Concepts:

*Write **your** psalm or prayer:*

Reverence

You are God most high
Almighty One
Pure bright holiness
Consuming fire

You are God most high
Knowing all
Aware of everything
Eyes penetrating

You are God most high
Everywhere present
Your light exposing
Revealing hearts

You are God most high
Loving Father
Wealthy in mercy
Wrath satisfied

You are God most high
Glorious Lamb
The Son Redeemer
Saving souls

You are God most high
Wonderful Counselor
Your Spirit transforming
Sustaining life

Write out and then meditate on / contemplate:

Psalm 7:10; Daniel 4:2,3; Luke 1:76-79

Journal Your Thoughts or Key Words/Phrases/Concepts:

*Write **your** psalm or prayer:*

Beware Deception

Oh, how deceived I can live!
Even with You as my Redeemer and Lord,
I am prone to lean on my own understanding
Convinced that some aspect of my transformation has concluded.

Oh, how deceived I can live!
Even with Your expert orchestration of my life,
I believe that I can know much better
Than Your authority established in wisdom over me.

Oh, how deceived I can live!
Even with Your unconditional love accessible to me,
I still surmise that to pick and choose
Whom **I** will love or not is a prerogative I can exercise.

Oh, how deceived I can live!
Even with Your magnanimous forgiveness of my offenses,
I am convinced it is permissible to shun
Those who have caused frustration or pain in my life.

Oh, how deceived I can live!
Even with Your blessings bestowed beyond my need,
I withhold and only carefully mete out
The wealth of resources within my possession to those in need.

Oh, how deceived I can live!
Even with Your example of volunteer loving-humility,
I allow my pride to override numerous chances
To expose my weaknesses and allow You to heal me.

Oh, how deceived I can live!
Even with You as my God and Counselor,
I forget how much I daily need You
To show me who I am and who I am **not**.

Oh, how truth-filled I can live!
Even with Your Spirit revealing my heart's reality,
I am not condemned but given great opportunity
For knowing freedom from deception's crippling of love.

Write out and then meditate on / contemplate:

Psalm 15; Psalm 119:29; Jeremiah 17:9,10; I Thessalonians 2:4

Journal Your Thoughts or Key Words/Phrases/Concepts:

*Write **your** psalm or prayer:*

Confession

Oh God
My only true Lord
I weary of wanting You yet chasing other things
I tire of words from my lips not matched by my actions
I cannot bear to hear my confession of negligence repeated
I am frustrated and stuck in the mire of my lazy faithless ways

Oh God
My only true Lord
I cry out to You to rescue me from my foolish entanglement
I want You because you are worthy of being fully wanted
I desire to praise You in word *and* deed to protect the glory of Your Name
I ache for freedom in obedience because You have freely forgiven

Oh God
My only true Lord
Thank You for granting faith to one such as me
Thank You for forgiving this wayward child
Thank You for transforming me patiently
Thank You for trusting me as a steward of Your love

Write out and then meditate on / contemplate:

Psalm 32:5; Psalm 38:15-18; Isaiah 6:5-7; Romans 3:25

Journal Your Thoughts or Key Words/Phrases/Concepts:

*Write **your** psalm or prayer:*

Weariness

I need to close my eyes and feel sun soaking a glow into my face
I need to have warm wind gently wrap my whole body 'round
I need my skin to tingle excitedly with heat
I need my lungs to inhale air of an invigorating new season
I need my feet engulfed by sun-kissed sand
I need deepest corners of my soul refreshed by wave's lingering mist
I need to open my arms and dance to a bird's favorite song
I need time of intimacy with my God underneath a smiling blue sky
                              It's been a heart's long winter

Write out and then meditate on / contemplate:

Psalm 105:2-4; Jeremiah 31:25; II Thessalonians 1:6,7

Journal Your Thoughts or Key Words/Phrases/Concepts:

*Write **your** psalm or prayer:*

Divine Purpose

Long ago
        In Your heaven You said
                Set them apart
So, for such as time as this
You have given us
Life and breath and everything else

Though You have given these to all men
                Yet we are set apart
And as such You determined
Our exact time for life and
Exactly where we should live

Your infinite wisdom and love
                Has set us apart
Not by merit of our own
But only by merit earned on our behalf
By our precious Jesus

Your Son's death, resurrection, forgiveness
                Sets us apart
In accordance with the measure of faith
You've given us to be for You
Daily, living, loving sacrifices

As Your chosen ambassadors and servants
                We have been set apart
Equipped with Your armor for battle
Against the devil's schemes and unseen forces
To take our stand and be found standing after all

May then Your purpose for us
        As set apart
Be accomplished that we might help lead
Those seeking and reaching for You
To be found by You, rescued, and set apart too

Lord of wonder and grace, increase
        Those set apart
That together by Your Spirit in us
We can worship and adore You with our lives
Showing more souls Your marvelous salvation

Write out and then meditate on / contemplate:

Psalm 40:9-11; Acts 17:26,27; Ephesians 6:10-13

Journal Your Thoughts or Key Words/Phrases/Concepts:

*Write **your** psalm or prayer:*

True Freedom

In confession and repentance there is freedom
In submission and humility there is freedom
In weakness and lack of control there is freedom
In tears and brokenness there is freedom
In relinquishing demand and manipulation there is freedom
In Your law and Your Word there is freedom
In choosing forgiveness and love there is freedom
In wrestling and battle there is freedom
In perseverance and endurance there is freedom

Freedom from the slavery of self
Freedom from the claustrophobia of addiction
Freedom from the pressure of constant acting
Freedom from the frenetic desire to be always right
Freedom from the oppression of comparison
Freedom from the bitterness of disappointments
Freedom from blindness to Your transforming work
Freedom from the error of preconceived notions
Freedom from doubting the truth of Your love

Freedom allows Your Spirit to teach us to love each other deeply
Freedom allows Your Spirit to open us to receive love
Freedom allows Your Spirit to heal our mind and heart wounds
Freedom allows Your Spirit to show us Your heart and mind
Freedom allows Your Spirit to enable us to stand against the enemy
Freedom allows Your Spirit to push us beyond comfort and familiarity
Freedom allows Your Spirit to speak to and through us whenever **You** want
Freedom allows Your Spirit to soften our hearts with compassion for others
Freedom allows Your Spirit to make us grateful for Your generosity to us
Freedom allows Your Spirit to give boldness to speak Your great Name

Write out and then meditate on / contemplate:

Psalm 119:45; II Corinthians 3:17; Galatians 5:22,23; I John 1:9

Journal Your Thoughts or Key Words/Phrases/Concepts:

*Write **your** psalm or prayer:*

Warfare

Though my soul knows praise to the Lord
Yet bubbling up from within are bursts of burden.
Though my soul knows praise to the Lord
Yet the arrows of the enemy hiss near my bowed head.

Abruptly I am called from my bowing state
To engage in the battle waging around me,
Thrusting me to stand, at times bewildered,
In the center of an other-worldly skirmish.
I am overwhelmed at the magnanimity of the war.
What can **I** do?!
What impact can the Sword in **my** hand make?
My heart's eyes stare, gaping at the grand struggle on all sides.
The eyes of hungry, empty souls gaze up at me;
their desperation growing while yet becoming numb to it.
Often unaware of the death-lock grip around them,
the enemy fights with horrific ferocity to maintain his hold.
Beyond my comprehension is how I could possibly
have been recruited for this army, this assignment.
I am then shaken by Truth out of my stupor.
I was a soul fought for by the brute force of Love Eternal,
Rescued from the icy clutches of hell's dominion.
I am now added to the never dying rescue squad,
Fending off sinister forces and schemes to
Find those wounded and bruised by darkness' abuses.
I must find others reaching out a shaky hand from among the dying,
Begging for escape, in order to partake themselves in the King's army.
My Rescuer supplies me with strength, protection, and skill.
So, I will ask Him for whatever I need in this battle.
He, my Supreme Master and Commander
Trains me to deftly wield the Sword I have been given and
To defend the ground He's placed me on.

I need not lose heart at the preposterous idea that
The whole war is mine to fight.
He, the Great and Love-defending Warrior, rides on
Paving the way to follow Him to
His ultimate and final victory over all.

Yes, my soul knows praise to the Lord.
His laud on my lips is my battle cry.
Yes, my soul knows praise to the Lord.
No enemy of His will succeed in drowning it out.

The battle is the Lord's!
Victory is His!
Praise be to Him!
Always and forever, amen!

Write out and then meditate on / contemplate:

Psalm 18:30-35; I Timothy 6:12; I John 5:4,5

Journal Your Thoughts or Key Words/Phrases/Concepts:

*Write **your** psalm or prayer:*

Promises, promises

All around are those who take a heart
to give a promise
only to break the promise
and the heart

Men who know You taste the goodness of Your heart
then taste "success"
only to abuse success
and Your heart

The enemy deceives men in their hearts
with a counterfeit promise
always breaking the promise
and hardening hearts

Lord we cry out to You to break hard hearts
to lead to repentance their souls
so You may heal their souls
and their hearts

Lord we cry out to You to rebuild hearts
and make new the minds
then guard the new minds
and the hearts

Lord You have asked us for our whole hearts
to give Your eternal promise
never to break Your promise
or crush our hearts

Write out and then meditate on / contemplate:

Psalm 33:4; Proverbs 20:25; Ecclesiastes 5:5; James 5:12

Journal Your Thoughts or Key Words/Phrases/Concepts:

*Write **your** psalm or prayer:*

Unforeseen Storm

Darkness suddenly surrounded me
I could not recognize the place I stood
No light could be seen by my eyes
Thick storm clouds enveloped my being
My breathing grew forced from the oppression
Rain burst out in torrents
Wind whipped against me
Trapped in its midst
There was nothing I could do
  So I sat down and waited
  I waited for You
The whirlwind knocked me
    stung me
    wounded me
Yet I lifted my head, my hands
Crying out Your Name
  Your Name alone
When You came
It was not as I'd imagined
  You did not lift me out
  You did not take me away
  You did not still the wind
  You did not halt the rain
Instead
  You sat down with me
  You took my hand
  You stayed with me
  You let me cry
  You held me in my pain
  You tended my wounds
  You waited too
In time… the sky brightened

Surroundings became familiar
My eyes took in light once more
The storm clouds floated off and faded away
Sky became blue and light
Sunshine warmed me
I breathed a weary sigh of relief
I got ready to stand up
Ready from this place to move
Then I realized
        You still held my hand
        Still there was You
        You stood up first
        Lifted me to my feet
        Raised my chin and
        On my forehead kissed me
I searched Your face, Your eyes
Could I find where such kindness came from
To command the storm away would have been easier for both
To walk away and not endure
Yet You chose the more difficult way for both
To show me the real heart of You

Write out and then meditate on / contemplate:

Psalm 40:11-13,17; Psalm 71:20; II Corinthians 12:8-10

Journal Your Thoughts or Key Words/Phrases/Concepts:

*Write **your** psalm or prayer:*

"Tranquil Newborn" Original artwork by Andrea Jerozal
www.simplyhisstudiollc.com

New Child Lullaby

hush my little love
sleep in peace
sleep in peace
hush my little love
sleep in peace

with end of sun comes end of day
we loved and learned the time away
now bubble bath and jammies warm
then good-night kiss in loving arms

hush my little love
sleep in peace
sleep in peace
hush my little love
sleep in peace

God is here He keeps you safe
just as He does when you're awake
close your eyes our little dear
rest well and know Jesus is here

Jesus says
hush my little love
sleep in peace
sleep in peace
hush my little love
sleep in peace

Write out and then meditate on / contemplate:

Psalm 8:1,2; Psalm 127:3,4; John 16:21

Journal Your Thoughts or Key Words/Phrases/Concepts:

*Write **your** psalm or prayer:*

Little Child Lullaby

Little eyes so full of light
Little laugh and smile bright
Little hugs so full of love
Little tasks to be proud of

Little heart so full of emotion
Little legs always in motion
Little one so full of trust
Little hands that tightly grasp

Little mind so quick to learn
Little knowledge of adult concerns
Little adventures in imagination
Little songs of own creation

Little words so bare and felt
Little looks to make hearts melt
Little moments so cherished now
Little memories forever endowed

Write out and then meditate on / contemplate:

Psalm 37:25,26; Psalm 139:2-6; Mark 10:13-16

Journal Your Thoughts or Key Words/Phrases/Concepts:

*Write **your** psalm or prayer:*

Tween Lullaby

Rest,
Young One.
This day's been full of care.
Much to learn, much to do.
Of new things you are aware
Yesterday you never knew.
Now rest.

Rest,
Young one.
Each day you change and grow.
New knowledge, new skills.
Applying what you now know
With both brain and will.
Now rest.

Rest,
Young one.
Today's had choices to make.
In your heart, in your mind.
Reputation or faith at stake
Decisions of character kind.
Now rest.

Rest,
Young one.
Your parents' hearts still with you.
As you come, as you go.
Here to listen and pray you through
No matter your life's tempo.
Now rest.

Rest,
Young one.
Tomorrow's concerns will wait
For your effort, your care
To determine their weight
In your young life's affairs.
Now rest.

Rest,
Young one.
Let your mind and body ease.
God has you, you know.
He guides you with Spirit breeze
So in this moment – let go.
And rest.

"Middle School XC" – original artwork by Andrea Jerozal
www.simplyhisstudiollc.com

Write out and then meditate on / contemplate:

Ecclesiastes 11:9; Psalm 71:5-7; Isaiah 40:30,31; II Timothy 2:22

Journal Your Thoughts or Key Words/Phrases/Concepts:

*Write **your** psalm or prayer:*

Orphan

Oh God
You see...
His heart cries
    Yet without visible tear fall
He gathers up his pain each morning
    Sobbing only through music
    Through angry outbursts
    Through athletic pursuits
He searches for a safe place
    A relief
    An oasis
Where his tears can freely spill
    To soothe the desert of his hurt

Oh God
You see...
Her broken dreams are locked away
    Where no one knows they exist
Notes to a song begun beautiful in youth
    Now float unconnected in discord.
    No melody.
    No rhythm.
    No meaning.

Oh God
You see...
She used to hold him
    She whispered her undying love to him
She embraced him when he hurt
    Until the pain went away
She was the one he trusted
She had youth and beauty to admire
She had comfort in her eyes

Oh God
You see…
She got distracted
She dropped his heart
    Letting the pieces just lie there
She walked away
She left him stranded
    In a whirlwind of
    Disappointment and confusion
She couldn't help him
    Find his way
She was now the source
    Not the comfort
    Of his pain
She hurt him more than anyone
She is his mother

Write out and then meditate on / contemplate:

Psalm 10:14; Isaiah 1:17; Isaiah 49:15; I John 3:1

Journal Your Thoughts or Key Words/Phrases/Concepts:

*Write **your** psalm or prayer:*

Refugee

The Lord is near.
The Lord is here.

Foreign territory
Chaos
Long journey
Exhaustion
Horror witnessed
Trauma
Familiar gone
Loss

Suspicious eyes
Caution
Culture shock
Ache
Haunting memories
Weeping
Odd surroundings
Stress

Friends scattered
Lonely
Need help
Scared
Strangers assist
Relief
Home provided
Exhale

The Lord is near.
The Lord is here.

New language
Struggle
Nuances missed
Vulnerable
Pronunciation challenge
Embarrassed
Persevere learning
Weary

Must provide
Pressure
Kids' school
Nervous
Connections made
Comforted
Routines created
Hopeful

Adapting daily
Relaxing
Grief surprises
Cry
Making friends
Optimistic
Helping others
Empowered

Ease comes
Settled
Celebrate again
Joy
Community participant
Belong
Home here
Grateful

The Lord is here.
The Lord is near.

Write out and then meditate on / contemplate:

Deuteronomy 10:17-19; Psalm 146:9; Zechariah 7:10; Ephesians 2:12

Journal Your Thoughts or Key Words/Phrases/Concepts:

*Write **your** psalm or prayer:*

Find Me

We in our finite world
Seek to tune in to a radio station
That is music to our ears and hearts.

So You, Oh Majestic Lord
Seek to tune in to souls on earth
That bring music to Your ears and heart.

You search from Your heavens, Oh God
For sounds transmitting Your eternal frequency
Do Your ears and heart recognize songs from me?

Or does my self-indulgence, Oh Merciful,
Create static to block tunes of
This life broadcasting praises to You?

I panic to think that You, Oh Lord,
Would pass me by as one in whom
You can't detect a melody of life-lived worship.

May I not be foolish to believe, Oh King,
That church or group attendance produces
A signal strong enough for Your notice.

Instead refine and purify me, Oh Holy One
To kill off the noise that crowds out my
heart and mind's transmission of love for You.

Make my life, Oh Living Redeemer,
The clear and strong vibe proclaiming a
Heart of radical love and service to You.

And may I be humble, Oh Father,
To receive the favor of Your Presence
Ever tuned to be communicated through me.

Write out and then meditate on / contemplate:

I Chronicles 28:9; Psalm 139:23; Jeremiah 17:10; Hebrews 4:13

Journal Your Thoughts or Key Words/Phrases/Concepts:

*Write **your** psalm or prayer:*

Exposed

Unexpected challenges expose my soul…
    Weak creatures, helpless beings
    Surface deep-seated selfishness

    Sick puppies, needy babies
    Disclose hidden agitation

    Life changes, new seasons
    Reveal controlling desires

    Diverse personalities, different backgrounds
    Expose unforgiving demands

    Unfulfilled expectations, thwarted hopes
    Announce anger-fixed judgments

    Intense emotions, mounting guilt
    Crack appealing facades

    Surprising disappointments, unforeseen tragedy
    Uncover frail faith

    Continual trials, recurring irritations
    Unearth poor perseverance

    God's Spirit, His eyes
    Breach unknown secrets

Write out and then meditate on / contemplate:

Psalm 51:9-12; Proverbs 19:11; James 4:8; II Corinthians 7:10

Journal Your Thoughts or Key Words/Phrases/Concepts:

*Write **your** psalm or prayer:*

Surprising Joy

Unexpected cheer brings joy to my soul…
    Children's laughter, cuddly puppies
    Bring spontaneous giggles

    Encouraging notes, surprising gifts
    Lighten daily routine

    Warm breezes, open windows
    Revive stale aspirations

    Forgiveness granted, grace extended
    Relieve sin-weary regret

    Relationships mended, friendships restored
    Renew love's hope

    Help offered, services rendered
    Humble silly pride

    Unexpected blessings, divine interventions
    Invigorate supernatural expectations

    Warm hugs, affectionate kisses
    Kindle outward perspective

    Jesus' love, redemption purchased
    Frees chained devotion

"Brothers" – original artwork by Andrea Jerozal
www.simplyhisstudiollc.com

Write out and then meditate on / contemplate:

Psalm 62:5; Psalm 145:8-10, 21; II Corinthians 13:11

Journal Your Thoughts or Key Words/Phrases/Concepts:

*Write **your** psalm or prayer:*

Grace

Grace is who You are
Your identity is not separate from grace
Grace originates with You
Your supply of grace is more than its need
Grace is given because of You
Your generosity to grant grace doesn't diminish
Grace comes from Your heart
Your desire is for grace to be received
Grace harmonizes all Your attributes
Your holiness is not compromised by bestowing grace
Grace exemplifies Your amazing patience
Your absolute forgiveness is undeserved
Grace reaches vilest offences through Jesus
Your redemption is the path of grace

Write out and then meditate on / contemplate:

Psalm 103:8-13; Isaiah 33:2; Ephesians 2:8,9; Romans 8:32

Journal Your Thoughts or Key Words/Phrases/Concepts:

*Write **your** psalm or prayer:*

Trinity

Holy are You
Mysterious Trinity
King of Fatherhood
Prince of Peace
Highness of Helping

Holy are You
Almighty God
Master Mind
Creative Power
Unending Sustainer

Holy are You
Forever Holy
Reigning Ruler
Loving Redeemer
Patient Teacher

Holy are You
Most High
Heaven's Owner
Heaven's Pathway
Heaven's Companion

Write out and then meditate on / contemplate:

Psalm 104:33,34; Luke 3:22; II Corinthians 3:14; Ephesians 2:17,18

Journal Your Thoughts or Key Words/Phrases/Concepts:

*Write **your** psalm or prayer:*

The Great Rescue

We forever will sing of the Great Rescue
No, not a fairy tale - it's real and true
A story of love continuing now
Until all nations join together and bow
Before the feet of the Savior gallant
Our ever-deserving Substitute valiant

Our souls by loneliness and fear enslaved
Indulged in all we grasped for and craved
Unable to see Love before our eyes
Seduced we were by the father of lies
Wasting away from our lust and desire
Being swallowed to hell, sucked into filth and mire

And when the enemy thought success was sure
An eternity of aloneness and regret secured
Boasting triumph over we fools unaware of our fate
Nearly condemned forever to hell's locked gate
Our Hero of heaven in the form of a man
Snuck into our midst with an unexpected plan

Paradise peeked through clouds to announce His birth
Unkempt outsiders first acknowledged His worth
Son of Eternal One and humble virgin was He
Cloaked in earth's dust and clay and poverty
Hidden in plain sight till time was just right
For the next phase of rescue from our sin-corrupt plight

Baptized in earth's water, affirmed from on high
His public life anointed by His Spirit-dove from the sky
He looked into the ashamed and touched the rejected
He healed the afflicted and embraced the neglected
His Word spoke authority to free souls enslaved by sin
Declaring woe to the self-righteous, sure they were "in"

Then it was time

Betrayed, framed to appear dangerous and guilty
Publicly dishonored, crowds hated Him without thinking
No advocate, no defense, no ease from the pain
He vulnerably, willingly, endured violence and shame
Battered and punished beyond recognition
His blood dripped to the dirt, then this life He relinquished

It was finished

God's enemy laughed and jeered a victory chant
Believing salvation doesn't happen when dead, it can't
Mankind would be doomed forever to defeat
While the snake could go on to oppress, hate, cheat
This enemy gloated and reveled in death
But then
God's Son inhaled *eternal resurrection breath*

Now sin's power is overthrown here and hereafter
Jesus glorified on His throne amidst worship and laughter
His Spirit possesses His children of faith, gives them gifts
Life together, forever, begins while still on earth they exist
The Father is satisfied, our debt paid in full by His Son
Now His adopted can be transformed and become one

We ever will sing of the Great Rescue
No, not a fairy tale – it's real and true
A story of love continuing now
Until all nations join together and bow
Before the feet of the Savior gallant
Our ever-deserving Substitute valiant

Write out and then meditate on / contemplate:

Psalm 18:6,7; II Corinthians 6:1,2; Ephesians 2:4,5; Hebrews 10:5-7

Journal Your Thoughts or Key Words/Phrases/Concepts:

*Write **your** psalm or prayer:*

Wrongly Accused

Consider the pain of a lover
Falsely accused of betrayal
No truth to the indictment
Yet forced to carry blame and
punishment for a wrong
never committed
No - only faithfulness and devotion
Have been loved and lived
Toward the beloved

What sorrow and rejection
Felt in not being believed
For what is true
How we must grieve You
O Lord
When in our hearts
We brazenly, carelessly
Sentence You unwittingly
To the punishment we deserve
By charging You guilty of so many
Attributes that are contrary
To Your true character

Write out and then meditate on / contemplate:

Psalm 18:30; Deuteronomy 32:4; Job 40:2, 7,8; II Corinthians 5:21

Journal Your Thoughts or Key Words/Phrases/Concepts:

*Write **your** psalm or prayer:*

Where?

Sucked into a vortex of exhaustion
And weakness, I wonder –
Where are You?
Pushed to my emotional and physical limit
I have become afraid of myself –
Where are You?
Patience is frail and self-control failing
The anger bursts up suddenly –
Where are You?
Crying to You for help and relief because
I know there is no other place to turn –
Where are You?
I continue to be pressed and pushed
Wondering if You ignore my pleas –
Where are You?
As I scream in silence for You to intervene
Things get worse –
Where are You?
I hear You whisper "I am here"
But I continue to struggle –
Where are You?
Why can't you be here in the way
I **want** You to be here –
Where are You?

Write out and then meditate on / contemplate:

Psalm 88:11-13; Lamentations 2:19; Luke 18:7,8; Hebrews 12:1-3

Journal Your Thoughts or Key Words/Phrases/Concepts:

*Write **your** psalm or prayer:*

Best

You are God
Jesus You are King
You have planned
Only best things
Rich or poor
Well or ill
Happiness or grief
Only **good** is Your will

There is a melody of praise
The arias of truth
Sung from deep within
About the wonder of You
Even in silence
Chords of worship
Emerge until the mind
Finally submits to hear
And join in

There is a music of strife
From the enemy's flute
Flattering tunes
That deceive about You
Notes of false comfort
Played for silent pain
Lure the weary heart
To falter and give in

But **no**

You are God
Jesus You are King
You have planned
Only best things
Rich or poor
Well or ill
Happiness or grief
Only **good** is Your will

Write out and then meditate on / contemplate:

Psalm 23:1-6; Romans 12:2; Ephesians 5:17

Journal Your Thoughts or Key Words/Phrases/Concepts:

*Write **your** psalm or prayer:*

Community

without one another
the enemy isolates us
and lies to us unchallenged

without one another
our pride inflates us
with no measure against reality

without one another
emotions would choke us
truth blocked from freeing

without one another
empathy evades experience
hurting hearts go uncomforted

without one another
Your trinity never existed
no God to love and save us

Write out and then meditate on / contemplate:

Psalm 133:1-3; Ecclesiastes 4:9-12

Journal Your Thoughts or Key Words/Phrases/Concepts:

*Write **your** psalm or prayer:*

Dying Young

(in memory of carol ann)

A violent birth
Life too few years
Delighting and maturing
Then gone

The violent good-bye
Ripped away from life
From loved ones
From me

The violent heartache
Waiting for God's wisdom
To make sense
To comfort

The violent reality
Intruding upon common apathy
Is limited mortality
Is fragility

The violent eternity **if**
Rejecting You in humanity
For fading pleasures
For vanity

Or
The peaceful eternity
Loving You in humanity
With unshaken faith
With devotion

The peaceful acceptance
Farewell to a friend
Knowing heaven embraces
Knowing eternal communion

Write out and then meditate on / contemplate:

Psalm 126:4-6; John 11:32-36

Journal Your Thoughts or Key Words/Phrases/Concepts:

*Write **your** psalm or prayer:*

Unborn Life

Oh Lord, when You began to knit a soul in my womb
what made You stop?
What is to become of the gasp of life my body nurtured
for such a short time?
Oh Author of life, who makes no mistakes
what was right about this?
How is Your Name to be praised by one whose voice
was never enabled?
Oh Eternal Breath of hope for all,
Why withhold Yourself from innocence?
How can it be that the force of my grief cannot will
this small soul to life?
Oh Gracious and Compassionate One,
are You angry with me?
Why deprive my arms and breast of nurturing
this wee body whose name You know?
Oh God, could You really wait no longer
for this tiny one to be with You?
Will I in Your presence one day meet the face
of one never meant to be?

Write out and then meditate on / contemplate:

Jeremiah 1:5; Psalm 22:9,10; Psalm 139:13; Luke 1:44

Journal Your Thoughts or Key Words/Phrases/Concepts:

*Write **your** psalm or prayer:*

Worship?

I stand with many who sing You songs of praise
And yet I know You receive more than words
You look to see what is in my heart not just on my lips
To find what You will accept as genuine worship

I stand with many who sing You songs of holiness
And I tremble to think of Your holy presence
Thunderously insulted by what careless hearts perceive as love
While falling woefully short of what You know true love to be

I stand with many who sing You songs of worship
And am ushered before You on Your throne
Under Your gaze where I cannot even pretend to hide
All the distractions and sinful desires I've recently caressed

I stand with many who sing You songs of love
Knowing nothing I can scrape together covers the nakedness of who I am
I can only cling to trust in the blood of Jesus hoping
He has already clothed me in His white robes of forgiveness

I stand with many who sing You songs of adoration
Aching in my heart for and yet trembling in awe for
The day my soul is released from this body
And in Your presence true, untainted songs will indeed be sung

Write out and then meditate on / contemplate:

Isaiah 29:13; Psalm 145:17-21; James 1:26,27; I John 3:16-18

Journal Your Thoughts or Key Words/Phrases/Concepts:

*Write **your** psalm or prayer:*

Child's Heart

In the heart of a child there resides unguarded emotion
Expectation of response to persistent requests

In the heart of a child there resides love's resilience
Forgiveness eagerly granted for want of love

In the heart of a child there resides unending curiosity
Excitement over each and every discovery

In the heart of a child there resides simple friendship
Invitation to come along and have fun

In the heart of a child there resides swelling adoration
Admiration for examples of kindness, confidence, and care

In the heart of a child there resides craving for warmth
Affection desired from family and elders

In the heart of a child there resides faith in what is not seen
Imagination of invisible realities come alive

In the heart of a child there resides all these that God loves:
Expectation, forgiveness, excitement, invitation, admiration, affection, imagination

In the heart of a child there resides what God desires in all His children:
Unguarded emotion, love's resilience, unending curiosity, simple friendship, swelling adoration, craving His warmth, faith.

"Sweet" – original artwork by Andrea Jerozal
www.simplyhisstudiollc.com

Write out and then meditate on / contemplate:

Psalm 119:9-11; Jeremiah 32:38-41; I John 5:2

Journal Your Thoughts or Key Words/Phrases/Concepts:

*Write **your** psalm or prayer:*

In Progress

Though perpetually unfinished
My soul aches for completion
Though continually in motion
I wish for everything to be still
Though the news blares terror
I hope to anchor home in peace
Though enemies scheme destruction
Love anyway vows to win
Though promised eternity
The temporal dominates my attention
Though all from this life must pass
I am reluctant to accept death
Though strength fails me
His Spirit renews me
Though days pass
God provides all for now

Write out and then meditate on / contemplate:

Psalm 103:2-5; Psalm 143:4-8; Galatians 6:9

Journal Your Thoughts or Key Words/Phrases/Concepts:

*Write **your** psalm or prayer:*

So True

Isn't it the truth? Someone will fiercely hold you to a high standard while granting generous grace to themselves.

Isn't it the truth? Some days will fall apart at the seams no matter how organized and planned you've been.

Isn't it the truth? Some people have a way of causing pain in the area of your heart you thought had been healed.

Isn't it the truth? Sometimes those precious little ones you'd give your very life for uncover selfish impatience.

Isn't it the truth? Someone can unexpectedly change the way you have perceived them thus far.

Isn't it the truth? Some days don't seem to have enough hours to meet the demands glaring at you.

Isn't it the truth? Some people will never understand you no matter how vulnerable and articulate you are.

Isn't it the truth? Sometimes you fervently pray and believe, yet tragedy strikes and your heart is broken to bits.

Isn't it the truth? Someone can make you laugh in the most inappropriate situation or moment.

Isn't it the truth? Some days renew your trust in hope and love by sweet surprises that pop up.

Isn't it the truth? Some people inspire admiration and imitation in the way they accept, forgive or are resilient.

Isn't it the truth? Sometimes you are just tired of rebelling or of image management and you finally surrender.

Write out and then meditate on / contemplate:

Psalm 34:9-14; Proverbs 18:1,2; Ecclesiastes 8:15; II Corinthians 7:2-4

Journal Your Thoughts or Key Words/Phrases/Concepts:

*Write **your** psalm or prayer:*

Loss

Fog
Heaviness
Unreachable ache
Hearing truth
Unable to absorb
Can't be still
Body wishing to run
How can this be?
Just a moment ago…

Wait
No
Not yet
Oh God
Let me rewind
Live it again
Not ready for this
Can't let go yet
How can this be?
Just a moment ago…

Inseparable
Together
Now alone
So quiet
Head is spinning
Heart is breaking
The weight of grief
Crushing from inside out
How can this be?
Just a moment ago…

Faith
Prayer
Answered no
Hope reshaped
No choice now
Breath once held
Can only weep uncontrollably
Relentless throbbing within
How can this be?
Just a moment ago…

"Remembered" – original artwork by Andrea Jerozal
www.simplyhisstudiollc.com

Write out and then meditate on / contemplate:

Isaiah 61:1-3; II Samuel 1:26; Psalm 31:9,10; Psalm 34:18; John 16:20-23

Journal Your Thoughts or Key Words/Phrases/Concepts:

*Write **your** psalm or prayer:*

Overwhelmed

Oh God
In Your presence
Without Jesus
I would be **doomed**
The sin carried in this body
Stuck in my mind
Stagnant in crevices in my heart
Would cause You (without Jesus)
Immediate disgust and
To act in repulsion
These words do not speak harshly of You
I am the one deserving
The full momentum of harshness

YOU are holy
You are ALL that is right
You are blindingly BRIGHT with purity
You are UNSTAINED beauty
You are UNMISTAKEN in ANY judgement
You are PRECISE in all wisdom
You are LOVE undiluted
I am overwhelmed I can be forgiven

Write out and then meditate on / contemplate:

Psalm 51:4; Psalm 79: 8,9; Micah 7:18; Acts 13:38,39

Journal Your Thoughts or Key Words/Phrases/Concepts:

*Write **your** psalm or prayer:*

Birthday Psalm

Today I remember
I stand accountable
For being granted life

Life breathed into me
Life knit together in divine intricacy
Life of days
Life planned
Life with good works prepared in advance to do
Life for God

In an unseen speck
The Unseen One embeds
Unseen genes, DNA, personality
Purpose

Today I remember
I stand accountable
For being granted life

Life including epic failures
Life of complicating me-focus
Life containing incalculable wasted moments
Life falling ever short of Divine plans
Life efforts crumbling in weakness
Life squandered on self

In unseen hopeless moments
The Unseen One spots
A speck of faith and embeds
Forgiveness, invitation
Renewed purpose

Today I remember
I stand accountable
For being granted new life

New life breathed and death overcome
New Life retracing original intention
New Life redeeming time
New Life walking steps beyond imagination
New Life discovering paths to introduce God to others
New Life of purpose pointing only to Him

In unseen cosmic reality
The Unseen One embeds my
Speck of redeemed life into
Eternity and His ever-after
Kingdom purposes

Today I remember
I stand accountable
For being granted life

Life grappling with present day genocide and horror
Life fighting the destruction of competition for significance
Life battling to trust Him even beyond the scope of my own obedience
Life fending off life-sucking entertainments and comforts
Life struggling in prayer for mercy for those loved, known, and unknown
Life clashing with death…to dreams, to precious ones, to preconceived purpose

> Feeling almost silly to have faith that life after the death will be better
> Life *with* **You** - whether yet here or in heaven

In unseen wrestling and trusting
You, Unseen One, embed my
Struggle into promised victory
Joys beyond anticipation
Ecstatic reality of being with You

Today I remember
I stand accountable
For being granted life
Twice
By the grace of Jesus

Forever –
Beyond my sin
And ever –
Beyond today's pain
And ever –
Beyond what I can't ever understand
And ever –
Washed clean in Your presence
And ever –
Jesus' atoning blood mine to claim
And ever –
Amen

Write out and then meditate on / contemplate:

Psalm 71:6; Psalm 143:8-10; Isaiah 12:2; John 3:3-6; II Timothy 3:14,15

Journal Your Thoughts or Key Words/Phrases/Concepts:

*Write **your** psalm or prayer:*

Heaven's Not Here

How much we may miss having access to much in this world
How shrunken and shriveled our imaginations
How little we truly know of God's heart and power

We who are rich are in grave danger
We who are rich are not defined as "blessed" by wealth alone
We who are rich are set up for deception as to what will finally satisfy

Material luxuries all can burn
Material status falsely puffs up
Material security is an unsound foundation

The stuff of earth does not last forever
The stuff of earth can rob us of true living
The stuff of earth can enslave, not free

Friends, worldly riches are a lame substitute for eternal joy
Friends, worldly riches are blinding many to their own desperate soul need
Friends, worldly riches are not the best to be aspired to in this life

This is not heaven

We may glimpse a preview of heaven in a tropical place
We may glimpse a preview of heaven when wealth reminds us God owns all
We may glimpse a preview of heaven in moments of peace and comfort

We will *miss* heaven if we set our hearts on those things

Heaven is sometimes *better* seen in the generosity of the poor
Heaven is sometimes *better* seen in the faith of the poor
Heaven is sometimes *better* seen in the hugs and gratitude of the poor

Jesus came from heaven and chose to be poor
Jesus came from heaven and chose to befriend the poor
Jesus came from heaven and was more easily recognized as Savior by the poor

Wealth is not evil – only hearts fixated on it
Wealth is not evil – only ambitions trying to hoard it
Wealth is not evil – only minds obsessed with it

To whom much is given, much responsibility is expected
To whom much is given, much generosity toward Kingdom work is anticipated
To whom much is given, much humility and genuine gratitude is required

Write out and then meditate on / contemplate:

Psalm 49:12-20; Luke 6:20; I Timothy 6:17-19

Journal Your Thoughts or Key Words/Phrases/Concepts:

*Write **your** psalm or prayer:*

Now

Can't erase what's past – it's already recorded
Can't control the future – it's already in motion

In this moment here and now
I breathe deeply, pray, and wait

Wait…for His Spirit intervention in the perfect storm
Wait…for His Word to shed light ahead of the next step
Wait…for peace to reach beyond what I think I understand

Can't erase what's past – it's already recorded
Can't control the future – it's already in motion

In this moment here and now
I breathe deeply, pray, and wait

Write out and then meditate on / contemplate:

Psalm 37:7-11; Psalm 130:5,6; Ecclesiastes 3:15; James 5:7,8

Journal Your Thoughts or Key Words/Phrases/Concepts:

*Write **your** psalm or prayer:*

Not Dead Yet

My eyes open
I am breathing
I've awakened to a new day
Though yesterday's troubles linger
In this moment there is distance…
Just enough to catch a new-mercy breath
Once I am in motion all will catch up to me
So in this brief stillness I allow these minutes to remind me
Life is Yours to give and I am still in possession of it
No matter this day's burdens You already knew You'd be here with me
Nothing in this day is surprising to You or beyond what You believe I can endure with Your help
What dies today, though I struggle and mourn, is a deposit into Your economy of resurrection newness
My heart, my outlook, my affections, my mind-life, my faith all ache and groan through trials
Yet
Become means by which You transform me to one more recognizable as Yours
I can cling to you with all I am in my most desperate of times
With praise to Your Name, I will marvel at the new me emerging
In Your mind this is closer to the me You intended all along
Pain endured can result in miracles beyond imagination
Your Son is proof
Almighty God You are

Write out and then meditate on / contemplate:

Psalm 9:9,10; Psalm 32:6-8; James 1:2-5

Journal Your Thoughts or Key Words/Phrases/Concepts:

*Write **your** psalm or prayer:*

Together

See…the flowers of the earth grow
Colors that individually and together paint our earth
Colors that individually and together bring delight
Colors that individually and together fragrance the wind
There is no one superior color or flower
Each brings its own vital display and joy
There is no flower or color fully complete outside the existence of the others

Look…the birds of the air abound
Winged species that individually and together entertain we humans
Winged species that individually and together waddle and soar
Winged species that individually and together keep ecosystems balanced
There is no one superior winged creature or bird
Each brings its own role and sense of awe
There is no winged creature set apart as best of all from the whole of the others

Look up… observe the array of stars
Lights that individually and together sparkle as limitless diamonds
Lights that individually and together guide and direct generations
Lights that individually and together are set into endless formations
There is no one singularly superior star
Each contributes its light and beauty from the expanse with plenty of room for all others
There is no star whose significance exists outside the community of other stars

God has created these and more
God has looked and seen and called **all** these good

Now… look around
See

Notice…all souls surrounding you live on Divine breath
Souls that individually and together reflect the image of their sole Creator
Souls housed in flesh and DNA not exactly replicated anywhere
Souls living in varied skin and eye and hair colors
There is no exclusively accepted variety of human soul
Each soul bursts forth the unique craftsmanship of its Maker
There is no one living soul more worthy of His great attention than another

Consider…the evil human souls have fallen prey to
Evil that rejects God as their imaginative, singular Creator
Evil that lies about God's intrinsic nature of pure justice
Evil that refuses to be content with love over favoritism
There is no single person favored most by God
Each soul is identically valued in His sight, offered equal opportunity to follow Him
There is no human being excluded from God's open invitation to accept His Gospel

Write out and then meditate on / contemplate:

Psalm 150:6; Luke 12:27; Romans 2:7-11; I Corinthians 15:39-41; James 2:8,9

Journal Your Thoughts or Key Words/Phrases/Concepts:

*Write **your** psalm or prayer:*

Grief Delayed

It came.
I began to think it wouldn't.
It seemed ok that it hadn't.
I thought about it sometimes.
It never entirely left my thoughts.
I knew it yet lingered.
It wafted like mist out of sight.
I sensed but didn't fully feel.
It was pushed back at the start.
I couldn't help it.
It wasn't the only loss of the moment.
I was already grieving.
It added to sadness but,
I needed time to revisit it separately.
It had not yet seemed the right moment.
I wondered if that time would ever come.
It had been years of wondering.

It came.
I was immersed in good things.
It was not invited or sought.
I had other things needing my energy.
It did not fit here.
I was simply living, loving, serving.
It took advantage of an unexpected opening.
I had no idea it would sneak in.
It was off my radar, so I thought.
I took one usual breath in, and with the next breath I was knocked out.
It was not convenient or timed nicely.
I thought, "NO way! Not NOW!"
It didn't matter…control was lost.
I was overcome and could barely breathe.

It undid me and there was no going back.
I was simply left to go through it.
It took me out at the knees without seeing it coming.
I struggled inside at the unfair surprise.
It required me to dance with it though I'd been wounded.
I was sad and unsure of this choreography.
It did not feet safe or comfortable.
I sighed and chose to take each step as they came.

I have Divine love thankfully.
It can lead me to gentle and secure places.
I have somehow managed to not completely collapse.
It holds my one hand and nods to me to also hold His.
I will one day tell of heartbreak healed.
I look forward to that completion.
It came.
I accept it.

Write out and then meditate on / contemplate:

Psalm 22:4; Ecclesiastes 7:2; Matthew 2:18

Journal Your Thoughts or Key Words/Phrases/Concepts:

*Write **your** psalm or prayer:*

Soul Talk

Oh my soul
So much stress and
Turmoil within.

Have you forgotten
Your Make ever with you
Your Lover ever for you?

Oh my soul
So much weight and
Burdens bearing.

Have you forgotten
Your Lord to rejoice in
Your God who calms storms?

Oh my soul,
So much churning and
Fear consuming.

Have you forgotten
Your Savior has evil defeated
Your Jesus who IS Conqueror?

Oh my soul,
So much to pray and
Petition honestly.

Have you forgotten
Your God to thank
Your Abba to trust?

Oh my soul,
So much to confess then
Peace returns.

Remember now
Your Maker ever with you
Your Lover ever for you!

Write out and then meditate on / contemplate:

Psalm 43:5; Psalm 52:5-8; Psalm 116:7; Matthew 11:25; Luke 1:46-49

Journal Your Thoughts or Key Words/Phrases/Concepts:

*Write **your** psalm or prayer:*

Enemy Intention

the **ENEMY** comes
    to **STEAL**

truth	whispering lies
	distorting perceptions
	parading counterfeit
	masquerading importance
love	promoting falsehood
	instilling fear
	severing connection
	hardening hearts

    to **KILL**

peace	pointing fingers
	stirring suspicion
	preserving pride
	raising self-doubt
hope	punishing kindness
	deceiving innocents
	laughing coldly
	teaching abandonment

    to **DESTROY**

good	oppressing weakness
	oozing mockery
	deceiving friendship
	blatantly humiliating
life	suffocating desire
	crushing spirits
	murdering time
	annihilating purpose

Write out and then meditate on / contemplate:

Psalm 17:8,9; John 10:9,10; Ephesians 6:10-12

Journal Your Thoughts or Key Words/Phrases/Concepts:

*Write **your** psalm or prayer:*

Modern Advent

Hours of uncertainty.
Nearing days.

Days without peace.
Nearing weeks.

Weeks of angry protests.
Nearing months.

Months of struggle.
Nearing years.

Years of faith-clashing violence.
Nearing decades.

Decades of needing Jesus.
Nearing centuries.

When will He come again?
Come Lord Jesus.

Write out and then meditate on / contemplate:

Psalm 98:1-3; Matthew 24:27; I Thessalonians 4:16-18; Hebrews 9:27,28

Journal Your Thoughts or Key Words/Phrases/Concepts:

*Write **your** psalm or prayer:*

Ambush

In cheerful step with You
I learn trust, love, obedience.
Confidence and intimate knowledge grow
as I continue faith steps.
In unsuspecting moments I'm ambushed
from a dull panic within.
Accusations seep into my thoughts
and fear yawns awake.
Maybe obedience was just pride
so shame is necessary to humble me.
Perhaps rejoicing in knowing God
was premature assurance.
The path I thought was good
may leave me left out and humiliated.

NO – these are lies.

Forgive my weak heart and mind.
You God **are** trustworthy.
Your lovingkindness endures forever.
Through my weakness and failings
You are pleased to demonstrate
grace and redemption and transformation
in such a life as mine.

Write out and then meditate on / contemplate:

Psalm 31:14-17; John 8:44; Philippians 4:8; Revelation 12:10,11

Journal Your Thoughts or Key Words/Phrases/Concepts:

*Write **your** psalm or prayer:*

Restless

Perpetually unfinished
My soul aches for completion
Pressing on
My strength and resolve grow weak
Forever in motion
I struggle to be still
Lacking understanding
Your ways are not my ways
Refining my affections
I wriggle against Your design for me
Desiring control
Surrender is slow

Write out and then meditate on / contemplate:

Psalm 51:10-11; Philippians 1:6; Ephesians 4:11-13

Journal Your Thoughts or Key Words/Phrases/Concepts:

*Write **your** psalm or prayer:*

Identity

Are we not Masterfully Created and God-breathed, His Delight and His Image?
Are we merely Existing and Surviving, Unseen and Random?
Are we not Prince and Princess, Heir and Heiress?
Are we Stingy and Discontent, Struggling and Striving?
Are we not Man and Woman, Son and Daughter?
Are we Aggressor and Combatant, Driven and Insecure?
Are we not Brother and Sister, Beloved and Friend?
Are we Freelance and Unattached, Conquerors and Oppressors?
Are we not Family and Neighbors, Citizens and Community?
Are we meant to be Cut-throat and Mercenary, Narcissistic and Exploitive?
Are we not designed like a Snow Crystal and Fingerprint, Beautiful and Unique?
Are we Conceited or Disdainful, Vain or Loathing?
Are we not beneficiaries of Grace and Mercy, Reconciled and Forgiven?
Are we Vindictive and Bitter, Grudge-bearing and Spiteful?
Are we not born for Purpose and Value, Significance and Security?
Are we just Alive and Breathing, Here then Gone?
Are we not Ambassadors and Agents, Representatives and Advocates?
Are we Self-righteous and Sanctimonious, Autonomous and Prideful?
Don't we reflect our Creator and Father, our Redeemer and Wise Counselor
As Compassionate and Gracious, Slow-to-anger and Abounding-in-Love?
Do we live as though we belong to God's Enemy and Adversary, Betrayer and Deceiver
Imitating him to be Attractive yet Crafty, Charismatic yet Destructive?
No!
No More!
We **are** God's Workmanship and Special Possession, His Children and Ministers of Reconciliation.
We **are** to imitate Him and Him **alone**, in Words and Actions.
Let it be so.

Write out and then meditate on / contemplate:

Exodus 19:5; Psalm 100:1-3; Philippians 2:3,4; I Peter 2:9

Journal Your Thoughts or Key Words/Phrases/Concepts:

*Write **your** psalm or prayer:*

Friendship

Friendships inspire.
Fictional friends and real friends.
Anne Shirley and her dedication to bosom friend Diana.
C.S. Lewis and J.R.R. Tolkien's affinity for the Divine.
Han Solo and Chewbacca navigating space and conflict.
Paul Simon and Art Garfunkel bonded in musical expression.
Rory and Lane grew up together and changed but endured.
Magic Johnson and Larry Bird brought together through sport and knocking down societal barriers.
Anna's act of true love for her icy sister Elsa.
David and Jonathan's covenant of friendship until death.
Ruth and Naomi's choice to intertwine lives.
Daniel, Shadrach, Meshach, and Abednego's true faith allegiance in a strange land of foreign gods.
Jesus, Mary, Martha, and Lazarus knit together in mutual invitation and acceptance.
Paul, Priscilla, and Aquila living life together as family for God's Kingdom.

Friendships inspire.
Real life made livable.
Honest truth and honest encouragement.
Moments of laughter and moments of tears.
Sacrificial acts and sacrificial devotion.
Promises made and promises kept.
Creating experiences and creating memories.
Committed through ease and committed through conflict.
Forgiving when wrong and forgiving when dumb.
Empathy in triumph and empathy in grief.
Keeping secrets and keeping trust.
Freedom to be apart and freedom to be together.
Shared interests and shared ideas.
Encouraging each other's faith and encouraging each other's strengths.

Jesus' friendship inspires.
Then and now.
In friendship, He walked with.
In friendship, He talked with.
In friendship, He ate with.
In friendship, He was faithful.
In friendship, He was betrayed.
In friendship, He was tested.
In friendship, He loved.
In friendship, He rejoiced.
In friendship, He wept.
In friendship, He lived rightly.
In friendship, He sacrificed Himself.
In friendship, He forgave.

There is no greater friendship than that of Jesus.
Jesus offers the gift of His friendship.
Jesus gives us the gift of friends.
True friendship is one of life's greatest joys.

Write out and then meditate on / contemplate:

Psalm 85:8-11; Proverbs 12;26; Proverbs 18:24; John 15:13-15

Journal Your Thoughts or Key Words/Phrases/Concepts:

*Write **your** psalm or prayer:*

Kingdom Come

There seems to be no nation that claims You to be their hallowed God.
Some nations claim a different god.
Some nations battle over which god will be declared theirs.
Some nations claim no one god at all.

There seems to be no country loyal to our Father in Heaven.
Some countries claim loyalty to their current leader.
Some countries claim loyalty to leaders of the past.
Some countries claim loyalty to an overthrown leader.

There seems to be no ruling regime that seeks Your Kingdom.
Some ruling regimes seek to boost their own kingdom.
Some ruling regimes seek to overthrow opposing kingdoms.
Some ruling regimes seek to maintain a kingdom of status quo.

There seems to be no government pointing to You for forgiveness.
Some governments offer only punishment and no forgiveness.
Some governments are silent on where to find forgiveness.
Some governments rely on laws and courts to define forgiveness.

There seems to be few communities that wholly trust You for their daily provision.
Some communities rely on each individual to create their own daily provision.
Some communities rely on hushed, dishonest gain for daily provision.
Some communities rely on the government for daily provision.

People who revere You as God alone,
Who call You Father,
Who seek Your Kingdom,
Who humbly beg Your forgiveness,
Who request Your daily provision...
They are like roses of hope whose petals are scattered among the nations,

They are like dispersed seeds that have taken root and produce Spirit-fruit in many countries,
They are like heavenly windows blowing the breeze of Your Kingdom into ruling regimes,
They are like lamps that shine Your light of forgiveness to the peoples overseen by governments,
They are like honeybees providing a honeycomb of saving truth to people across earth's communities.

Meanwhile,
We pray:
Your Kingdom come,
Your will be done,
On earth,
As it
Is in
Heaven.

Write out and then meditate on / contemplate:

Psalm 33:8,9,12-15; Matthew 6:9-15

Journal Your Thoughts or Key Words/Phrases/Concepts:

*Write **your** psalm or prayer:*

Question Death

(In memory of Eric Hanson)

Death.
Permanent separation.
That word triggers dark dread.
That word pierces and pains.
That word.
That awful word.
Thoughts race toward loved ones.
Minds race to schedule completion.

Death.
It's too much.
Good-bye forever is too much.
Missing all that could be shared.
Missing the future potential.
Invisible memories.
Invisible remembrance.

Death.
Mourning the never again.
Wailing for the never again.
Not here.
Not with.
Unbearable the weight of absence.
Unbearable the loss of touch.

Death.
Starting small, a moment dies.
Starting small, an idea dies.
Then an anticipation dies.
Then an aspiration dies.
Even bigger a strategy dies.

Even bigger a loved one dies.

Death.
Life experiences death.
Life experiences loss.
Yet other life lives on.
Yet other life presses on.
Life holding its deaths.
Life mourning its losses.

Flowers die.
Pets die.
Expectations die.
Hopes die.
Plans die.
Dreams die.
Loves die.

Death.
How can there be joy?
How can there be meaning?
Why live?
Why breathe?
Where's the point?
Where's the reason?

Death.
A tulip's bloom - gone.
A tree's leaves - gone.
Grass withered.
Plants limp.
Green turned gray.
Full become empty.

Death.
Did you notice?

Did you see?
A bloom comes back again!
Trees burst with brilliance again!
Gray is chased out by vivid green!
Emptiness cannot push back new fullness!

Death.
Did you notice?
Did you see?
Separation from this earth is not finality.
Separation from this earth is a phase.
What follows is **life**!
What follows death is ***new* life**!

Death.
You may cause good-bye.
You may make us wait.
In faith, your effect is temporary.
In faith, hope for resurrection is not in vain.
Restoration awaits.
Perfection awaits.
And then...

Death.
You will die.
You will vanish.
Your influence cut off forever.
Your memory extinguished.
Finished.
Terminated.

Because **Life**...
Is Father, Jesus, Spirit.
Life...
Is His to give and give again.
Life ...

Life In Psalm

Unlike death with a beginning and an end.
Life …
God has no beginning or end.
Life…
Awe, joy, celebration.
Life…
Growth, love, devotion.
Life *again*…
Wonder, ecstasy, splendor!
Life *again* …
Worship, gushing gratitude, lavish love!
Life *again* …
Reunion, relationship, rejoicing!
Life *again* …
Uninterrupted peace and perfect never-ending relationship!

Yes, we will walk through the intensity of the grief death imposes.
No, we will **not** mourn deaths as if there is no hope.

Write out and then meditate on / contemplate:

Proverbs 11:7; I Corinthians 15:55; I Thessalonians 4:13,14

Journal Your Thoughts or Key Words/Phrases/Concepts:

*Write **your** psalm or prayer:*

Love Psalm

A man sees with his eyes, yes.
His heart is not absent.
He may envision romance and intimacy, yes.
His mind also contains vision of home.
Made of wood or brick perhaps, yes.
His desire is more a home of peace and trust.
A man will notice and note her figure, yes.
His sense will tell him if their values align.
He may burn from within for her nearness, yes.
His soul will yearn for her adoring respect.
Made of mystery and fragrance she is, yes.
His experience of her seems new daily.

A woman feels with her heart, yes.
Her eyes are not blind.
She may dream from youth of love, yes.
Her hope is for notice of her nobility.
Praying and waiting to create a family home, yes.
Her breath is held to be at home in his company.
A woman longs to be touched and held, yes.
Her ache from within is be valued for all she is.
She may imagine an enviable kiss of the ages, yes.
Her aspiration will be his honor of her to others.
Designed for strength and provision he is, yes.
Her triumph is to win his confidence and devotion.

Together a relationship comes into being, yes.
They learn and discover.
Together they may make plans, yes.
They comfort and adapt in the face of the unexpected.
Together forgiveness and sacrifice are learned, yes.
They rarely perceive the unfathomable depth of their union.

Together their bodies delight and unite, yes.
They engage in a bond only barely understood.
Together they may falter and get weary, yes.
They become friends with grace and serving.
Together God and family are pursued, yes.
They have the fruit of Divine blessing to enjoy eternally.

"Radiant" – original artwork by Andrea Jerozal
www.simplyhisstudiollc.com

Write out and then meditate on / contemplate:

Genesis 29:20; Proverbs 5:19; Ruth 3:11; Ephesians 5:25-28, 32

Journal Your Thoughts or Key Words/Phrases/Concepts:

*Write **your** psalm or prayer:*

In the End

Yahweh
Light
Love
Presence
Hope Realized

Yahweh
Majesty
Glory
Praise
Irrepressible Worship

Yahweh
Son
Lamb
Sacrifice
Wrath Satisfied

Yahweh
Elders
Martyrs
Saints
Jeweled Throne

Yahweh
Joy
Tenderness
Reward
Tears Banished

Yahweh
City
Home
Family
Exquisite Feast

Yahweh
Rivers
Trees
Vineyards
Endless Bounty

Yahweh
Gold
Pearl
Gemstones
Matchless Treasure

Yahweh
Fellowship
Community
Assembly
Forever Belonging

Yahweh
Life
Responsibility
Purpose
Unending Delight

Yahweh
Eternity
Radiance
Wonder
Everlasting Beauty

Yahweh
Yeshua
Ruach Elohim

Jehovah
Adonai
Shalom

Father
Son
Spirit

His Children
His Company
His Shelter

Infinite
Never Ending
Amen
Come Lord Jesus

Write out and then meditate on / contemplate:

Matthew 25:23; John 5:17; II Corinthians 5:1; Revelation 21:3,4

Journal Your Thoughts or Key Words/Phrases/Concepts:

*Write **your** psalm or prayer:*

Appendix

Life In Psalm	Suggested Playlist
Celebrate!	Psalm 118 – Shane & Shane
He Hears	God Who Listens – Chris Tomlin with Thomas Rhett
Awe	So Will I – Hillsong UNITED
Reverence	Your Great Name – Natalie Grant
Beware Deception	Boasting – Lecrae with Anthony Evans
Confession	Resurrecting – Elevation Worship
Weariness	Joy – For King & Country
Divine Purpose	Raise A Hallelujah – Bethel Music
True Freedom	Freedom Hymn – Austin French
Warfare	Made For This - Carrollton
Promises, Promises	Promises – Maverick City/TRIBL
Unforeseen Storm	My Only Hope – Gateway Worship
New Child Lullaby	Good Good Father – Chris Tomlin
Little Child Lullaby	The Blessing – Kari Jobe, Cody Carnes, Elevation Worship
Tween Lullaby	This Is Living – Hillsong Young & Free with Lecrae
Orphan	Daughters of Zion – The Porter's Gate
Refugee	Move – Jesus Culture
Find Me	Build Your Kingdom – Rend Collective
Exposed	Holy Water – We The Kingdom
Surprising Joy	Sing Wherever I Go – We The Kingdom

Grace	Take Me Into The Beautiful – Cloverton
Trinity	Echo Holy – Red Rocks Worship
The Great Rescue	No Rival – Crowder with JR
Wrongly Accused	Every Praise – Hezekiah Walker
Where?	My World Needs You – Kirk Franklin
Best	Smile – Sidewalk Prophets
Community	TOGETHER – For King & Country, Tori Kelly, Kirk Franklin
Young Death	40 – U2
Unborn Life	Trust In You – Lauren Daigle
Worship?	O Come to the Altar – Elevation Worship
Child's Heart	This Little Light of Mine – Addison Road
In Progress	Unstoppable – Toby Mac with Blanca
So True	Place of Freedom – Highlands Worship
Loss	Live On Forever – The Afters
Overwhelmed	Lift Your Head Weary Sinner – Crowder
Birthday Psalm	Jesus Loves Me – Shane & Shane
Heaven's Not Here	In Christ Alone – Passion w/ Kristian Stanfield
Now	I Smile – Kirk Franklin
Not Dead Yet	It's Not Over Yet – For King & Country
Together	Make Us One – Jesus Culture
Grief Delayed	I Am Not Alone – Kari Jobe
Soul Talk	Stand In Your Love – Bethel Music & Josh Baldwin
Enemy Intention	Not Today – Hillsong UNITED
Modern Advent	God Turn It Around – Church of the City

Ambush	Quiet – Elevation Rhythm
Restless	Tremble – Mosaic MSC
Identity	You Say – Lauren Daigle
Friendship	Wild – Local Sound
Kingdom Come	Our Father – Bethel Music
Question Death	When We Fall Apart – Ryan Stevenson
Love Psalm	Nearness of You – Norah Jones
In The End	Revelation Song – Gateway Worship